© **POSITIVE WORLD**
BY SANDEEP RAVIDUTT SHARMA

Table of Contents

Introduction IV

POSITIVE WORLD..1

© POSITIVE WORLD
BY SANDEEP RAVIDUTT SHARMA

Introduction

This book provides you with a list of **100 motivational quotes and thoughts** focussing mainly on improving your wellness quotient. Never give up even when your mind convinces you. Feed positivity to your mind and let the inspiration make you do things differently and win. Take the first step forward and keep going with a smile. The world awaits you with a bouquet of joy and happiness at the destination. I'm sure if you keep reading, referring, sharing these thoughts and quotes, you may derive inspiration and develop a good understanding of various business perspectives and facts.

"Avoid walking barefoot in the desert to create your footprints for others to follow. Do things which make sense for you first and then guide the world. With your good thoughts and deeds, create a positive world."

I sincerely hope, you will find this book amazing, interesting, rejuvenating, unique and constant source of inspiration.

Thank You and Happy Reading.

© POSITIVE WORLD
BY SANDEEP RAVIDUTT SHARMA

© Copyright 2018 Sandeep Ravidutt Sharma - All rights reserved.

In no way is it legal to reproduce, duplicate, or transmit any part of this document in either electronic means or in printed format. Recording of this publication is strictly prohibited and any storage of this document is not allowed unless with written permission from the publisher. All rights reserved. The information provided herein is stated to be truthful and consistent, in that any liability, in terms of inattention or otherwise, by any usage or abuse of any policies, processes, or directions contained within is the solitary and utter responsibility of the recipient reader. Under no circumstances will any legal responsibility or blame be held against the author / publisher for any reparation, damages, or monetary loss due to the information herein, either directly or indirectly. The author own all copyrights.

Legal Notice:
This book is copyright protected. This is only for personal use. You cannot amend, distribute, sell, use, quote or paraphrase any part or the content within this book without the consent of the author or copyright owner. Legal action will be pursued if this is breached.

Disclaimer Notice:
Please note the information contained within this book is for motivational, educational and knowledge sharing purpose only. Every attempt has been made to provide the reader accurate, up to date and reliable complete information. No warranties of any kind are expressed or implied. Readers acknowledge that the author is not engaging in the rendering of legal, financial, medical or professional advice. By reading this document, the reader agrees that under no circumstances the author / publisher is responsible for any losses, direct or indirect, which are incurred as a result of the use of information contained within this document, including, but not limited to, —errors, omissions, or inaccuracies.

If you have further questions, contact on
Tel: +919969256731
Email: sandeepraviduttsharma@gmail.com

Dedication

This book is dedicated to **Goddess Bhairavi**. In the Hindu religion, the Goddess Bhairavi represents divine anger and wrath which is directed towards impurities within us as well as to the negative forces that obstructs our spiritual growth. Bhairavi Mata is also called as **Shubhamkari** and does good things. She is often depicted in images as holding a book, rosary and making abhaya and varada mudra with her hands. She is fiercely protective, lending us wisdom and power, steadiness and clarity. She personifies light and fire, supporting us to reveal what we keep hidden and inviting us to explore our hidden mind and any secret darkness.

I hereby recite the following Bhairavi mool mantra...
"Om Hreem Bhairavi Kalaum Hreem Svaha"
And pray to **Goddess Bhairavi** for lending wisdom and power, steadiness and clarity in the life of my readers and the world. May Goddess Bhairavi protect us from negative forces along with removing impurities of our mind.

POSITIVE WORLD

© **POSITIVE WORLD**
BY SANDEEP RAVIDUTT SHARMA

Look back in life just to check how much distance you have covered so far, and motivate self to cover the remaining soon.

You can't teach someone to trust. Trust needs to be earned and felt by both the interacting parties.

© **POSITIVE WORLD**
BY SANDEEP RAVIDUTT SHARMA

Do not postpone the celebration of life even when the life journey is about to end.

© POSITIVE WORLD
BY SANDEEP RAVIDUTT SHARMA

During turbulent times don't start blaming this or that instead focus on the tide and ride over the current crises.

Your karma or deeds never gets lost in the universe. It comes back to you in some form or the other.

Gather courage to shed all the negative baggage of the past and sooner you will find TODAY showering a welcome smile at you.

Those who intend to achieve their dreams need to drive in reality.

Run away from anger as fast as you can.

Successful persons are those who do things today and never ever postpone it for the next day.

© POSITIVE WORLD
BY SANDEEP RAVIDUTT SHARMA

Be ready to welcome happiness, peace, prosperity, friendship, kindness, good health and blessings in your life.

Take the risk if you want to explore the unknown.

If opportunity doesn't knock your door. Don't wait for too long, take the first step forward to go and meet the opportunity.

It's hard to accept defeat and learn from mistakes. Those who can do both can win someday.

Reflection can create illusion while reality creates an impression. Go for reality.

© POSITIVE WORLD
BY SANDEEP RAVIDUTT SHARMA

The world waits to see you shine like the Sun in the Sky. You need to get up in time to perform and be a winner.

© **POSITIVE WORLD**
BY SANDEEP RAVIDUTT SHARMA

Change is inevitable. Embrace change in time with a positive attitude and kind heart.

Those who over estimate their own abilities fall flat someday. It's better to leave your estimation in the minds of those whom you serve with dedication.

© **POSITIVE WORLD**
BY SANDEEP RAVIDUTT SHARMA

Lead and motivate people today towards a better and promising tomorrow.

Trust the Lord and you will never lose.

God listens to one and all, and gives a helping hand when you take the first step forward with determination and good intentions.

Leadership is not a one day affair but a life-long commitment.

You really don't own anything in this world except your karma. So make an attempt to remove this fear of losing what you think you own.

Standing alone is fine if the cause is noble.

Find time to check facts before you decide to judge others.

Those who try to decimate others get buried in their own pit. Be good to one and all and goodness follows you wherever you go.

Yesterday was a good or bad day, you only can tell but can't change. Today very much depends on your affirmative actions and Tomorrow never comes.

Be the Change in this world and not the sundry change for a trader.

If you believe in speed don't attempt to walk fast instead run.

© **POSITIVE WORLD**
BY SANDEEP RAVIDUTT SHARMA

Your thoughts have got the power to change the world.

Stop reading stories of what you did in the past Focus on the present as you create stories for the future.

As you drown yourself into the ocean of knowledge, you get to learn how to swim in life and become a lifeguard for those who failed to learn.

Gather courage to face the world even if you have failed a number of times. Success only comes to those who persist and don't surrender or turn back.

Life behaves strangely every minute. When the response is favourable, you feel happy and in adverse times you blame it all on life. Remember life appears the way you have carved it on your own. So stop complaining instead act in time.

The obstacles clear the path when they find you dressing them as opportunities.

Each of us has got a different perspective. Try to understand and respect the perspective of the other.

Kind words create positive impressions.

© **POSITIVE WORLD**
BY SANDEEP RAVIDUTT SHARMA

You need to write first if you intend to read again.

© POSITIVE WORLD
BY SANDEEP RAVIDUTT SHARMA

As the day turns into the night, and you have few minutes for yourself. Remember the good moments of your day, slow down your thoughts and relax whereever you are. Do nothing for a while and it can recharge you for the next day.

Going forward look for opportunities matching your skills or with your innovative thinking create opportunities.

The pain is the mother of happiness. Face the pain with all your strength and deliver happiness with a smile.

Your first attempt is crucial as far as learning is concerned. Your second attempt can be a masterstroke as far as achieving success is concerned.

Follow your dreams with confidence in your abilities and positive actions.

Navigate your mind through the bylanes of wisdom, and you are sure to find the solution.

Time doesn't stop for anyone whether you act or react.

Courage makes full use of your strength in times of crisis.

You feel happy not when someone orders you to be happy, but when you enjoy freedom, achievement and is proud to be a kind human.

Self-discovery is not a one time act but it's for a lifetime.

No one can help a person who is painting black and white despite gifted with the rainbow of colours. Paint your life with colours of positivity and happiness.

Don't just count the money in your locker, count your good deeds and remember the countless blessings which you received due to your random act of kindness.

© **POSITIVE WORLD**
BY SANDEEP RAVIDUTT SHARMA

The drop of rain is just water when it falls into the lake, becomes nameless when it falls into the soil, referred to as Waves when it meets the ocean, and is known as Pearl when it is conceived in an Oysters shell. The Universe or the Creator has dropped you into the lap of your earthly parents or guardians, who may be rich or poor, kind or cruel. But it has allowed you to do Karma and convert your own non-identity into a Diamond.

Sometimes instead of understanding genuine issues faced by others, we end up proving ourselves right.

You meet God every day but due to glasses of ego not able to recognise him.

Freedom ensures Victory.

Cherish your moments of joy.

© **POSITIVE WORLD**
BY SANDEEP RAVIDUTT SHARMA

Laughter challenges the environment.

When you are happy it shows up on your face. Never try to suppress but always express your happiness. It is infectious and can benefit others.

Freedom from worries is within sight when you focus on the solution.

You become what you think.

Appreciation can motivate the recipient towards excellence.

The good listener converts spoken words into Gold and not Dust.

Don't waste your time in striking out options rather focus on selecting one.

If the golden sun can sit down with the vast sea every evening to discuss. Why can't we put down our ego and live in harmony?

You can't hide when you grow tall in life. All your actions and reactions are in the public eye. Acting responsibly is the only way forward.

Your patience will be tested each time whenever you are close to your destination. Have patience...You are just a step away from achieving your goals.

The storm of thoughts in the ocean of life seems to be a threat but in fact is a way to test your faith and patience by the creator.

Happiness multiplies when shared.

Never let your mind wander in the dark lanes of tomorrow. Think positive.

The challengers of the future are learners of today.

Success cannot be decided only on the money you possess. Your attempt to create the smile on faces of others after wiping out tears count more.

Those who suppress their likeness lives in isolation and a lonely life. Share your likeness and invite positivity all around.

You can unearth the treasure of Love and happiness by staying committed.

You start your day with a smile and work to bring the smile on the face of others as well.

© POSITIVE WORLD
BY SANDEEP RAVIDUTT SHARMA

Scrutinize the facts before you pass a verdict else innocent ones may suffer.

To avoid misunderstanding, you need to first try to understand what the other person has to say.

If the world seems to be going upside down and beyond your control. Try reversing your position and check whether syncing with the world helps the cause for a greater good.

Arrogance has to kneel down someday. Get rid of it in time.

Your voice becomes more impactful when conveyed through silence and non-violence.

Get out of your comfort zone if you intend to do something worthwhile in your life.

Some of us think only about our own self and wish people appreciate our work, ideas and thoughts. But at the same time, their ego stops them to appreciate the work of others. Appreciate others and be thankful to one and all.

Attachments to material objects in life often write the story of pain and sufferings. With your devotion, get attached to the Lord and feel the bliss.

The seeker of truth has to keep trying no matter what he gets in the end.

Distraction comes your way not to stop you but to test how well you can focus.

Patience helps you to wait but mainly aims to make you calm in any kind of situation.

Grand salute to those who fought for our freedom and values. With courage and education, we can ensure freedom for one and all.

Blend your ideas with your Karma, and you can shine.

Reciprocate with love and affection for the one who makes you smile.

Always thank all those who have been supportive and corrected you every time you have faltered from the righteous path.

Instead of acting like a victim and gaining sympathy, it is better to take up the challenge and emerge as a victor.

© **POSITIVE WORLD**
BY SANDEEP RAVIDUTT SHARMA

Do the right things at the right time if you want to achieve success.

God gave us the brain and heart to take care of not just the mankind but the other beings as well. Be kind. Be human.

Golden Sun doesn't practice any kind of discrimination while it showers light on the entire world.

Do things differently to achieve your goals.

What you see may not be true always, so have patience for truth to reveal itself. No one can hide the truth for long.

Success stories are written only after one achieves success. Prepare yourself first to win.

You can skip using an elevator if fitness is your prime concern.

Leave your desk to know the world.

The pain and sufferings in our life are the greatest teachers. One is sure to remember the lessons learnt for a lifetime.

You can climb over all kinds of hurdles in life provided your willpower is strong and you believe in, 'Never say die' attitude.

Ask for it and get ready to receive abundance in your life.

Trying small is better than just thinking big.

www.ingramcontent.com/pod-product-compliance
Lightning Source LLC
Chambersburg PA
CBHW070803220526
45466CB00002B/530